T0390101

!NSP!RE

# BEYONCÉ

## BY JILL SHERMAN

AMICUS LEARNING

**Inspire is published by**
**Amicus Learning, an imprint of Amicus**
P.O. Box 227
Mankato, MN 56002
www.amicuspublishing.us

**Editor:** Ana Brauer
**Series Designer:** Kathleen Petelinsek
**Book Designer and Photo Researcher:** Emily Dietz

**Library of Congress Cataloging-in-Publication Data**
Names: Sherman, Jill, author.
Title: Beyoncé / by Jill Sherman.
Description: Mankato, MN : Amicus Learning, 2025. | Series: Inspire | Includes bibliographical references
    and index. | Audience: Ages 5–9 | Audience: Grades 2–3 | Summary: "Learn about global superstar
    Beyoncé and her accomplishments as a musician in this biography packed with photos and fact-filled
    text suitable for young readers. Includes a table of contents, glossary, further resources, and index" —
    Provided by publisher.
Identifiers: LCCN 2024012073 (print) | LCCN 2024012074 (ebook) | ISBN 9798892001014 (library
    binding) | ISBN 9798892001595 (paperback) | ISBN 9798892002172 (ebook)
Subjects: LCSH: Beyoncé, 1981—Juvenile literature. | Singers—United States—
    Biography—Juvenile literature.
Classification: LCC ML3930.K66 S54 2025  (print) | LCC ML3930.K66  (ebook) | DDC
    782.42164092 [B]—dc23/eng/20240315
LC record available at https://lccn.loc.gov/2024012073
LC ebook record available at https://lccn.loc.gov/2024012074

**Photo Credits:** Alamy Stock Photo/Brittany Smith, 8–9; AP Photo/Chris Pizzello, cover;
Getty Images/BEN STANSALL, 7, Houston Chronicle Hearst Newspapers, 10, Jeff
Kravitz, 19, Kevin Mazur, 4, 14, 18, 20, 21, Kristian Dowling, 17, Michael Caulfield
Archive, 13; Shutterstock/Roman Sigaev, 12

**Printed in China**

# Table of Contents

Beyoncé fans are called the BeyHive.

# Queen Bey

Beyoncé is one of the biggest music stars today. When she takes the stage, it is clear she is in charge. Fans love how her music makes them feel strong and powerful. Beyoncé's groundbreaking music career has earned her the nickname Queen Bey.

# What's in a Name?

Do you know anyone else with the name Beyoncé? Likely not. Her name came from her mom's **maiden name**. Her full name is Beyoncé Giselle Knowles. She's so famous, most people just call her Beyoncé.

Beyoncé (right) with her mom in 2012.

Beyoncé (far left) got her start with a band she started with her friends.

# Search for
# Stardom

Beyoncé has a great voice. When she was young, she joined a singing group called Girls Tyme. In 1993, they performed on the TV show *Star Search*. They didn't win. So Beyoncé worked even harder.

**Destiny's Child in 1997. Left to right: LaTavia Roberson, LeToya Luckett, Kelly Rowland, Beyoncé Knowles.**

# Destined for Fame

The group didn't give up. They changed their name to Destiny's Child. In 1997, they got a record deal. Their songs soon became smash hits. Destiny's Child became one of the most popular female **R&B** groups.

**CHILDHOOD FRIENDS**
Beyoncé grew up with the original members of Destiny's Child.

# Going Solo

In 2003, Beyoncé took a risk. She made a solo album. Her voice was front and center. There was no denying it. Beyoncé was a true R&B **diva**. She recorded "Crazy in Love" with rapper Jay-Z. It was the first **single** on her album. In 2008, they got married.

**NOT THE END**
Beyoncé returned to Destiny's Child in 2004. They made one more album together.

Beyoncé sang at the 2003 Radio Music Awards.

Beyoncé did the famous "Single Ladies" dance at the 2013 Super Bowl halftime show.

# Going Viral

Beyoncé quickly rose to fame. Her music video for "Single Ladies" went **viral** online. Justin Timberlake, Joe Jonas, and even President Obama copied the **iconic** dance moves. The song hit the top of the music **charts**.

# Making Her Mark

Beyoncé makes the most of her stage time. She sang at the Video Music Awards (VMAs) in 2011. At the end of the song, she threw open her jacket. She was pregnant! Then, she performed at the 2016 Super Bowl. Beyoncé released a new song the day before. "Formation" was her song against racism.

In 2011, Beyoncé announced that she was pregnant after performing her song "Love On Top."

In 2018, Beyoncé and Jay-Z went on tour together.

# Musical Family

Beyoncé's sister, Solange, has her own music career. In 2018, Beyoncé and her husband Jay-Z made an album together. They called themselves The Carters. Jay-Z's real name is Shawn Corey Carter.

Beyoncé (left) dances with Solange at a music festival in 2014.

# Renaissance

Beyoncé's concerts are great fun! In 2023, Beyoncé started her **Renaissance** World Tour. She wore eye-popping costumes. Fans wore wild outfits, too! In 2024, Beyoncé released her first country album.

**RECORD HOLDER**
As of 2024, Beyoncé and Jay-Z are tied as the most nominated musicians in Grammy history.

Beyoncé sang songs from her album *Renaissance* during her 2023 tour.

# SUPER STATS

## BEYONCÉ KNOWLES-CARTER

**Birthday:** September 4, 1981

**Hometown:** Houston, Texas

**Children:** 3

## AWARDS THROUGH 2024

**Grammys:** 32

**Billboard Music Awards:** 27

**MTV Video Music Awards:** 29

## ALBUMS

*Dangerously in Love* (2003)

*B'day* (2006)

*I Am...Sasha Fierce* (2008)

*4* (2011)

*Beyoncé* (2013)

*Lemonade* (2016)

*The Lion King: The Gift* (2019)

*Renaissance* (2022)

*Cowboy Carter* (2024)

## THE CARTERS ALBUMS

*Everything Is Love* (2018)

# GLOSSARY

**chart** A ranking of the most popular music.

**diva** A glamorous and successful female performer with a strong personality.

**iconic** Something that is widely known or easily recognized.

**maiden name** A person's last name before marriage.

**R&B** Rhythm and blues, a type of music.

**renaissance** A period of great artistic activity.

**single** A song usually released before the album.

**viral** Quickly and widely spread through social media.

# READ MORE

Isdahl, Nansubuga Nagadya. **Beyoncé.** New York: Abrams Books for Young Readers. 2021.

Kawa, Katie. **Beyoncé: Making a Difference through Music.** KidHaven Publishing, 2022.

Moss, Caroline. **Work It, Girl: Beyoncé Knowles: Rule the Music Scene like Queen.** Quarto Publishing Group UK, 2021.

# ON THE WEB

**All Music**
https://www.allmusic.com/artist/beyonc%C3%A9-mn0000761179

**Official Website of Beyoncé**
https://www.beyonce.com/

# INDEX

## About the Author

Jill Sherman writes books about pop stars, baby animals, and robots. She loves that writing allows her to research and learn about new topics. In addition to writing books, Jill sews her own clothes, creates crossword puzzles, and codes in JavaScript.

She listened to all of Beyoncé's music while writing this book.